YOU'RE WEIRD, SIR!

Peanuts Parade Paperbacks

1. Who's the Funny-Looking Kid with the Big Nose?
2. It's a Long Way to Tipperary
3. There's a Vulture Outside
4. What's Wrong with Being Crabby?
5. What Makes You Think You're Happy?
6. Fly, You Stupid Kite, Fly!
7. The Mad Punter Strikes Again
8. A Kiss on the Nose Turns Anger Aside
9. Thank Goodness for People
10. What Makes Musicians So Sarcastic?
11. Speak Softly, and Carry a Beagle
12. Don't Hassle Me with Your Sighs, Chuck
13. There Goes the Shutout
14. Always Stick Up for the Underbird
15. It's Hard Work Being Bitter
16. How Long, Great Pumpkin, How Long?
17. A Smile Makes a Lousy Umbrella
18. My Anxieties Have Anxieties
19. It's Great to Be a Super Star
20. Stop Snowing on My Secretary
21. Summers Fly, Winters Walk
22. The Beagle Has Landed
23. And a Woodstock in a Birch Tree
24. Here Comes the April Fool!
25. Dr. Beagle and Mr. Hyde
26. You're Weird, Sir!

YOU'RE WEIRD, SIR!

by Charles M. Schulz

Holt, Rinehart and Winston/New York

PEANUTS comic strips by Charles M. Schulz
Copyright © 1981, 1982 by United Feature Syndicate, Inc.

Published by Holt, Rinehart and Winston,
383 Madison Avenue, New York, New York 10017.

Published simultaneously in Canada by Holt, Rinehart
and Winston of Canada, Limited.

First published in book form in 1982.

Library of Congress Catalog Card Number: 82-81658

ISBN: 0-03-062099-6

First Edition

Printed in the United States of America

10 9 8 7 6 5 4 3 2 1

© 1965 United Feature Syndicate, Inc.

ISBN 0-03-062099-6

The Sea

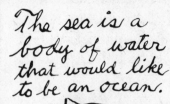

The sea is a body of water that would like to be an ocean.

I think.

The sea is filled with many wonderful creatures.

There are also many wonderful creatures on top of the sea.

If they aren't careful, however, they can end up on the bottom of the sea with the other wonderful creatures.

Which may not be so wonderful.

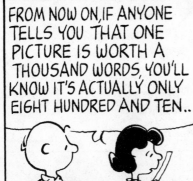

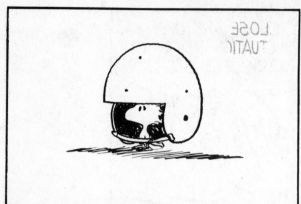

WHEN YOU'RE ON A HIKE LIKE THIS, MEN, YOU HAVE TO ANTICIPATE DIFFICULTIES

LIKE THIS GORGE, FOR INSTANCE..HOW DO WE GET ACROSS?

BEHOLD!

A BEAGLE BRIDGE!

DON'T LOOK DOWN, MEN...JUST MARCH RIGHT ACROSS...

PEOPLE DON'T THINK ABOUT IT, BUT WHEN YOU'RE A BRIDGE, YOU GET LONELY AT NIGHT

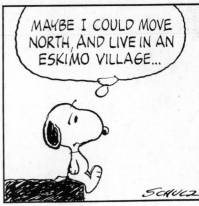

AND NOW WE'RE DOWN TO THE LAST TWO VALENTINES...

THIS ONE IS FOR "MY SWEET BABBOO" AND THIS ONE IS FOR "THE CUTEST OF THE CUTE"

WILL THE PERSONS TO WHOM THESE BEAUTIFUL VALENTINES ARE ADDRESSED PLEASE STEP FORWARD?

I WENT HOME!!

IT SEEMS TO BE ALMOST A MYSTERY...

WHY DO SOME OF US GET NO VALENTINES WHILE OTHERS GET MORE THAN THEY CAN COUNT?

YOU'RE RIGHT, CHARLIE BROWN...IT SEEMS TO BE A MYSTERY...

AND THOSE OF US WHO KNOW, WON'T TELL!

SCHULZ

IF WE EVER HAVE AN INK SHORTAGE, YOU'RE GONNA BE BLAMED!

THIS IS MY RAIN DANCE

THE NATIVES USED TO DO THIS WHEN THEY WANTED RAIN

THIS IS MY SUPPERTIME DANCE

IT DOESN'T ALWAYS WORK EITHER!

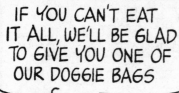

WOULDN'T IT BE SOMETHING IF THAT LITTLE RED-HAIRED GIRL CAME OVER HERE AND GAVE ME A KISS?

I'D SAY, "THANK YOU! WHAT WAS THAT FOR?" AND WOULDN'T IT BE SOMETHING IF SHE SAID, "BECAUSE I'VE ALWAYS LOVED YOU!"

THEN I'D GIVE HER A BIG HUG, AND SHE'D KISS ME AGAIN! WOULDN'T THAT BE SOMETHING?

WOULDN'T IT BE SOMETHING IF IT TURNED OUT THAT FRENCH FRIES WERE GOOD FOR YOU?

This is my report on Halley's comma.

HALLEY'S COMMA?

IT'S A VERY FAMOUS COMMA

HE PROBABLY WROTE HOME A LOT

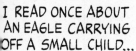

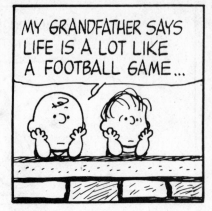

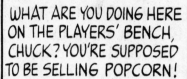

AHEM!

THIS IS MY REPORT ON "HANS BRINKER OR THE SILVER SKATES"

THE MAIN EMPHASIS OF MY REPORT WILL DEAL WITH THE STRANGE SECTION THAT BEGINS ON PAGE SEVENTY-TWO..

HERE WE HAVE THE STORY OF THE BOY WHO SAVED THE CITY BY PLACING HIS FINGER IN THE HOLE OF THE DIKE...

THUS, HE STOPPED THE LEAK THAT WOULD HAVE FLOODED THE CITY...HE WAS A HERO!

HOWEVER, WHAT IF THE BOY LOST THE USE OF HIS FINGER? COULD THE DOCTOR HAVE BEEN SUED FOR IMPROPER DIAGNOSIS?

AND WHAT IF THE BOY'S FAMILY BROUGHT A PERSONAL INJURY ACTION AGAINST THE CITY FOR FAILING TO PROPERLY MAINTAIN THE DIKE?

HAS ANYONE EVER THOUGHT OF THIS? ALL RIGHT, THEN, SUPPOSE WE..

MA'AM?

SIGH ANOTHER D MINUS..

THERE'S ONLY ONE PROBLEM WITH EATING IN THE RAIN...

IT TENDS TO COOL DOWN YOUR PIZZA

YOU KNOW WHAT I JUST SAW?

I CAN'T IMAGINE

SOME KID WAS ON A SKATEBOARD, AND HIS DOG WAS PULLING HIM ALONG THE SIDEWALK...

DO YOU WANT TO TRY IT?

THIS ISN'T EVEN CLOSE TO WHAT I MEANT

Dear Sweetheart, Thank you for your nice letter.

I'm glad you are enjoying your trip.

Stay well. Write again if you have time. Love, Snoopy

P.S. Don't break any leash laws.

IT'S A PHILOSOPHY, SIR...

IT SAYS THAT IF YOU DENY SOMETHING EXISTS, THEN IT DOESN'T EXIST

SORRY, MA'AM

YOUR "D MINUSES" DON'T EXIST!

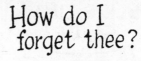

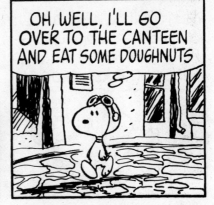

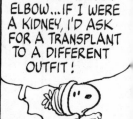

YOUR WRITING IS TOO STODGY, BIG BROTHER..YOU NEED TO WRITE WITH MORE FLAIR...LOOSEN UP...

THAT'S BETTER... SMUDGE WITH FLAIR!

HI, EUDORA... ARE YOU GOING TO SUMMER CAMP THIS YEAR?

I'M NOT SURE...

I WILL IF MY PARENTS CHAIN ME UP, PUT ME IN A BOX AND THROW ME ON THE BUS...

SEE YOU THERE

SCHULZ

THERE'S SOMETHING LONELY ABOUT A BALL FIELD WHEN IT'S RAINING...

WHAT MAKES IT LONELY, IS BEING THE ONLY ONE DUMB ENOUGH TO BE STANDING OUT HERE...

There are seven continents; Africa, Asia, Australia,

Europe, North America, South America and Aunt Arctica.

I'M GLAD YOU DIDN'T LEAVE HER OUT

WHAT DO YOU MEAN BY THAT?

I'LL NEVER GET A SCHOLARSHIP TO A BIG EASTERN COLLEGE WITH YOU BOTHERING ME!

BEAN BAGS ARE A BOON TO SULKERS

LIFE IS DIFFERENT FOR THEM

PEOPLE DON'T HAVE WINGS, SEE...

SO INSIDE THEIR TALL BUILDINGS THEY HAVE WHAT THEY CALL "ELEVATORS"

THEY'RE REALLY JUST BIG BOXES WITH A LOT OF BUTTONS...

IF YOU PUSH ONE BUTTON, YOU GO UP...

WHOOP!

IF YOU PUSH ANOTHER BUTTON, YOU GO DOWN..

WHOOP!

IN SOME BUILDINGS THEY HAVE "ESCALATORS" WHICH YOU STAND ON, AND...

KLUNK!

ACTUALLY, IT'S A LOT BETTER JUST TO HAVE WINGS...

HOW DO YOU GET EVEN WITH AN OCEAN?

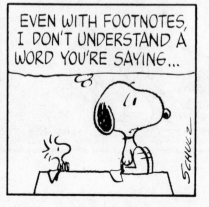

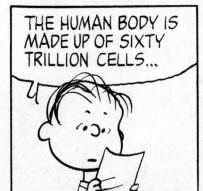

MARCIE, LOOK! THE BUTTERFLY HAS COME BACK! WHAT DO YOU SUPPOSE THIS MEANS?

MAYBE IT'S NOT AN ANGEL ANYMORE, SIR.

THAT'S TOO BAD...

BACK TO THE MINORS, EH?

?

WHO WAS THAT?

DON'T ASK

JOE PREPPY

DO YOU KNOW MUCH ABOUT LOVE, CHUCK?

PROBABLY NOT

WELL, IF A LIKES B, BUT B LIKES C WHO LIKES D AND E WHO BOTH LIKE A WHO DOESN'T EVEN KNOW THAT D EXISTS, SHOULD F TRY TO HAVE G TALK TO B SO E WILL KNOW THAT C LIKES D AND E, AND THAT C WILL POUND H IF SHE COMES AROUND AGAIN BUTTING IN?

MAY I THINK ABOUT THAT FOR A MINUTE?

SURE, CHUCK..IN THE MEANTIME, HERE'S ANOTHER ONE....SAY A PERSON HAS KIND OF A BIG NOSE, AND ANOTHER PERSON CALLS HER "BASEBALL NOSE," AND TELLS HER NOT TO GO NEAR THE BALL PARK 'CAUSE SOMEONE MIGHT AUTOGRAPH HER NOSE, SHOULD SHE BE OFFENDED?

WHAT DO YOU THINK, CHUCK?

G SHOULDN'T GET INVOLVED, AND AN AUTOGRAPH ON A NOSE WOULD PROBABLY WASH OFF...

YOU DON'T KNOW ANYTHING ABOUT LOVE, CHUCK!

PROBABLY NOT

SCHULZ

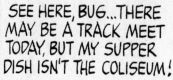

OH, YEAH? WELL, DOGS CAN DO LOTS OF THINGS THAT BIRDS CAN'T DO...

BIRDS CAN'T RIDE IN CARS WITH THEIR HEADS OUT THE WINDOW...

A DOG CAN STICK HIS HEAD OUT OF THE WINDOW AND LET HIS TONGUE AND EARS FLAP IN THE WIND LIKE THIS...

YOU KNOW WHAT WOULD HAPPEN IF A BIRD WAS IN A CAR, AND HE STUCK HIS HEAD OUT OF THE WINDOW?

THAT'S WHAT WOULD HAPPEN..

WHICH, NOW THAT I THINK ABOUT IT, DOESN'T PROVE VERY MUCH..

YES, MA'AM.. MORE THAN READY...

THEY'RE GONNA LOVE THIS, MARCIE!

THIS IS MY REPORT ON "WHAT I DID THIS SUMMER"... AT THE CONCLUSION, I WILL ANSWER QUESTIONS..

ONE DAY LATE IN THE SUMMER, I WAS LYING IN A MEADOW, WHEN SUDDENLY, A BUTTERFLY LANDED ON MY NOSE!

HA HA HA H HA HA HA HA HAHA

WELL, I DIDN'T WANT TO BRUSH IT AWAY BECAUSE I MIGHT HURT IT...

AFTER A WHILE I MUST HAVE DOZED OFF.. WHEN I OPENED MY EYES, THE BUTTERFLY WAS GONE!

YOU'LL NEVER GUESS WHAT HAPPENED... IT HAD TURNED INTO AN ANGEL, AND FLOWN AWAY!

HA HA HA HA HA HA HA HA

WELL, THIS WAS OBVIOUSLY A MIRACLE! I HAD BEEN CHOSEN TO BRING A MESSAGE TO THE WORLD!

WHAT WAS THIS MESSAGE I WAS TO BRING TO THE WORLD? AFTER MUCH THOUGHT, I DECIDED IT WAS THIS, "A FOUL BALL HIT BEHIND THIRD BASE IS THE SHORTSTOP'S PLAY!"

HA HA HA HA HA HA HA HA

MA'AM, IF IT'S OKAY WITH YOU, I'LL TAKE THE QUESTIONS AFTER SCHOOL OUT IN THE ALLEY BEHIND THE GYM

This is my report on the letter M, which is the thirteenth letter of our alphabet.

OR THE TWELFTH IF THE LETTER "J" IS OMITTED

IF WHAT?

F "J" IS OMITTED, THEN M" IS ONLY THE TWELFTH ETTER OF THE ALPHABET

WHY WOULD WE LEAVE OUT "J"?

"J" WAS FORMERLY A VARIANT OF "I"... IN THE SEVENTEENTH CENTURY IT BECAME ESTABLISHED AS A CONSONANT ONLY, AS IN "JULIUS" WHICH WAS ORIGINALLY "IULIUS."... THUS, "M" IS ONLY THE TWELFTH LETTER OF THE ALPHABET IF "J" IS OMITTED!

I CAN DO BETTER THAN THAT..

I'LL OMIT THE WHOLE REPORT!

SCHULZ

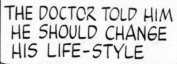

READ THIS, MARCIE...IT'S ALL ABOUT A SCHOOL FOR GIFTED CHILDREN

I'VE NEVER HEARD OF A SCHOOL BEFORE THAT GIVES YOU THINGS

I DON'T THINK IT MEANS THAT, SIR

I'D SETTLE FOR JUST A T-SHIRT

"ACE SCHOOL FOR GIFTED CHILDREN"... HOW ABOUT THAT, CHUCK?

JUST THINK...A SCHOOL THAT GIVES YOU PRESENTS! I'M GONNA APPLY!

ARE YOU SURE YOU'RE READING THAT RIGHT?

THE FIRST THINGS I'M GONNA ASK FOR ARE SOME NEW SKATES AND MAYBE A DART BOARD...

SHE WENT OVER TO A SCHOOL FOR GIFTED CHILDREN, CHARLES..SHE THINKS THEY'RE GOING TO GIVE HER THINGS...

I DON'T KNOW WHAT TO DO ABOUT HER, CHARLES.. SHE NEVER LISTENS...

CHARLES? ARE YOU THERE? WHO AM I TALKING TO?

IF I BARK, IT'LL SCARE HER TO DEATH...

YES, MA'AM..IF THIS IS THE SCHOOL FOR GIFTED CHILDREN, I'D LIKE TO ENROLL...

DO I THINK I'M GIFTED?

I'M NOT SURE

I USUALLY GET A FEW THINGS FOR MY BIRTHDAY AND FOR CHRISTMAS, BUT THAT'S ABOUT IT...

YES, MA'AM, I READ IN THE PAPER ABOUT YOUR SCHOOL FOR GIFTED CHILDREN

MY SCHOOL IS ALL RIGHT, BUT I LIKE YOUR APPROACH BETTER

IS THIS BAG GOING TO BE BIG ENOUGH FOR ALL THE GIFTS?

THESE ARE MY CLOTHING AND SHOE SIZES..IF YOU GIVE OUT ICE SKATES, I'D LIKE THEM ABOUT ONE SIZE SMALLER...

MISUNDERSTANDING? ISN'T THIS THE SCHOOL FOR GIFTED CHILDREN? AREN'T YOU GONNA FILL MY BAG WITH GIFTS?

BUT I THOUGHT... I WAS SURE THAT... AREN'T YOU... I MEAN... I...

OH, NO!

IF ANYONE ASKS FOR ME, I WAS NEVER HERE!

CHARLIE BROWN, HAS ANYONE EVER TOLD YOU THAT YOU WALK FUNNY?

YOU DON'T HAVE ANY RHYTHM! YOUR FEET POINT IN ALL THE WRONG DIRECTIONS..YOUR ARMS SWING THE WRONG WAY...

STAND UP STRAIGHT..NOW MOVE FORWARD...WALK THE WAY I TOLD YOU...

KLUNK!

I STILL THINK IT'S A MATTER OF RHYTHM..TRY IT AGAIN...

BONK!

HOW AM I GOING TO GET HOME?

KEEP WORKING AT IT.. I'VE DONE ALL I CAN

WHAT IN THE WORLD ARE YOU DOING?

THIS IS CALLED, "STARTING OVER RIGHT FROM THE BEGINNING"

SCHULZ

HEY, WHAT ARE YOU DOING?

YOU CAN'T JUST TAKE THINGS OUT OF THE REFRIGERATOR!

LOOK, IT SAYS HERE IN EXODUS, "THOU SHALL NOT STEAL"

DEUTERONOMY 25:4... "THOU SHALL NOT MUZZLE THE OX WHILE HE TREADS OUT THE GRAIN"

I DON'T SEE YOU TREADING OUT ANY GRAIN!

IT GOT ME OUT THE BACK DOOR

IN SOUTHWEST CAMEROON THERE ARE FROGS THAT WEIGH TEN POUNDS

THAT IS DEFINITELY NOT SOMETHING TO BE TOLD JUST BEFORE YOU GO TO SLEEP

SCHULZ

RATS!

IT'S IMPOSSIBLE TO SLEEP IF YOU THINK A TEN POUND FROG FROM SOUTHWEST CAMEROON MAY COME AND JUMP ON YOUR STOMACH...

PLEASE CLOSE ALL THE WINDOWS

SCHULZ

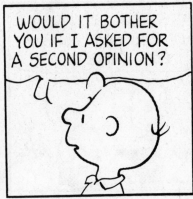

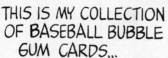

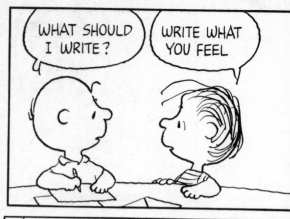

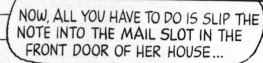

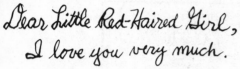

Gentlemen, Regarding the recent rejection slip you sent me.

I think there might have been a misunderstanding.

What I really wanted was for you to publish my story, and send me fifty thousand dollars.

Didn't you realize that?

DON'T COMPLAIN ABOUT THE RAIN... WE NEED RAIN..

WITHOUT RAIN NOTHING WOULD GROW, AND WE'D HAVE NOTHING TO DRINK!

SO NEVER COMPLAIN ABOUT THE RAIN

WHIMPER, BUT DON'T COMPLAIN

I HATE NOSE RAIN!

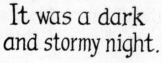

It was a dark and stormy night.

IF YOU'RE HAVING TROUBLE SELLING YOUR WORK, I'D SUGGEST A DIFFERENT APPROACH...

It was a stormy and dark night.

IF YOU WERE ON A CONCERT TOUR IN FAR-OFF PLACES, WOULD YOU CALL ME EVERY DAY?

NO, I'D NEVER CALL YOU

YOU'D PROBABLY WRITE THOUGH, WOULDN'T YOU?

NO, I'D NEVER WRITE TO YOU

BUT YOU'D PROBABLY SEND ME CUTE LITTLE POSTCARDS THAT WOULD SHOW WHERE YOU WERE STAYING AND SIGHTS YOU HAD SEEN...

NO, I WOULD NEVER SEND YOU A POSTCARD

BUT IF YOU HAPPENED TO MEET SOMEONE IN A HOTEL LOBBY WHOM WE BOTH KNEW, YOU'D PROBABLY TELL HIM TO SAY "HELLO" TO ME WHEN HE GOT BACK HOME, WOULDN'T YOU?

WHO KNOWS? I MIGHT...

I KNEW YOU'D MISS ME!

SCHULZ

WHAT ELSE SHOWS MORE DEVOTION?

TO GET UP IN THE MIDDLE OF THE NIGHT, AND TAKE A BLANKET OUT TO A FREEZING FRIEND...

NOTHING, UNLESS, IN YOUR SLEEPY CONDITION, YOU PLACE IT ON THE WRONG END!

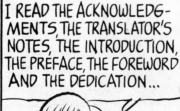

YES, MA'AM, I'VE BEEN READING THE BOOK...

WELL, NOT ACTUALLY THE BOOK YET...

I READ THE ACKNOWLEDG-MENTS, THE TRANSLATOR'S NOTES, THE INTRODUCTION, THE PREFACE, THE FOREWORD AND THE DEDICATION...

IT'S BEEN UPHILL ALL THE WAY!

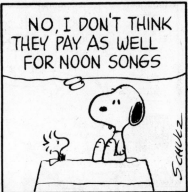

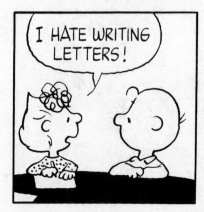